P9-DGX-512

The AUTISM ACCEPTANCE BOOK

Being a Friend to Someone with Autism

by Ellen Sabin

and _____

WRITE YOUR NAME HERE

WATERING CAN® PRESS

WATERING CAN®

Growing Kids with Character

When you care about things and nurture them,
they will grow healthy, strong, and happy, and in turn,
will make the world a better place.

All rights reserved. No part of this book may be used or reproduced in any
manner whatsoever without prior written permission of the publisher except
in the case of brief quotations embodied in critical articles and reviews.

Several website addresses (URLs) are provided in this book as resource references.
The publisher does not maintain these sites, all of which were active and valid
at the time of publication. Please note that over time, URLs and/or their content
may change. We regret any inconvenience this may cause readers.

Text and illustrations © 2006 by Ellen Sabin

WATERING CAN is a registered trademark of Ellen Sabin.

Written by Ellen Sabin
Illustrated by Kerren Barbas
Designed by Heather Zschock

ISBN-13: 978-0-9759868-2-0
ISBN-10: 0-9759868-2-1
Printed in China
By Best Tri Colour Printing & Packaging Co.

Website address: www.wateringcanpress.com

Dear _____,

Because you are such a nice, caring, and kind person, I am giving you this **AUTISM ACCEPTANCE BOOK**.

With this book, you will learn about autism and some of the different qualities of people with autism.

You will see that, like you, people with autism have their own special skills and challenges. And, just like you, they want to be accepted and understood.

People with autism may not always act the exact ways that you expect, but if you take time to understand them, you will get to learn new things and make new friends.

From, _____

Some "thank-yous"

- To Brian and Tricia Kelly for asking me to write this book and for giving me the opportunity to learn so much in the process.

- To my sister, Debby Sabin Kanzer, and others like her who work with children with special needs and show them devotion, patience, and understanding every day.

- To Lynn Koegel and Rita Gardner for their expert reviews and edits; Karen Margulis London, Peter Bell, Lee Grossman, and Alison Singer for their encouragement, input, and support.

- To all of the parents and teachers of children with autism who provided feedback, insight, and input that shaped this book and its message.

A NOTE TO ADULTS

Autism is a growing problem that afflicts thousands of children every year. Children with autism face many challenges and obstacles. These children will have an easier time navigating the world if the people in their lives take the time to understand them.

Children who do not have autism live in a world that is made up of people who are different from each other in all sorts of ways. The best way to teach children tolerance and acceptance is by encouraging them to take the time, and make the effort, to understand and respect others. That way, they will learn empathy and compassion and will learn to treat people the ways they would like to be treated themselves.

When children learn about people with autism they will be supporting their peers, making new friends, and ultimately strengthening their own character.

We hope this book will engage and inspire them.

It will give them an opportunity to explore and experience how it feels to be different, and how nice it feels to be understood and accepted. It will introduce them to the challenges faced by people with special needs.

This activity book will support their personal journey toward appreciating and respecting people's differences.

Table of Contents

What is
The AUTISM ACCEPTANCE BOOK?

Welcome to Your AUTISM ACCEPTANCE BOOK!

What do all your friends, family, teachers, and the people in your community have in common?

They are all different from one another!

Everyone is different in some ways, which is great, because this is what makes us all unique and special.

When people seem different from you, the best thing to do is to try to understand them and find out what is special about each of them.

The **AUTISM ACCEPTANCE BOOK** will help you learn more about people who may seem different than you because they have autism.

- It will teach you about autism and many of the things that are difficult for people with autism.

- It will show you that we are all different and help you understand why people with autism may sometimes act differently than you do.

- It will help you imagine how things might feel for people with autism.

- It will let you figure out ways to be understanding, accepting, and even helpful to people with autism.

- You will see that when you make an effort to understand people, you will find their special qualities. That means that anyone can become your friend if you take the time to understand him or her. When you do this, you will build all kinds of new and valuable friendships.

What are you waiting for? Turn the page and get started! ●●●▶

How does
The AUTISM ACCEPTANCE BOOK work?

First

You think about how everyone is different from each other and how nice it feels when people accept and include each other.

Next

You learn about autism—what it is, how it affects people, and how some things can be difficult for people who have autism.

Then

You explore how and why your friends with autism may act differently than you do. You can even try to imagine some of the things that are hard for them and how things might feel to them.

And Once you understand how your friends with autism may feel, you can think about ways to be thoughtful and supportive of them.

Then You can even do things with your classmates and friends—like raise money to donate for autism research or teach others about autism. You can also share what you've learned with others and show them how important it is to try to understand, accept, and include everyone.

REMEMBER: This is YOUR book. Along the way, you can keep a journal, write notes, and collect ideas about autism, being a good friend, and accepting others.

Take a Walk in Someone Else's Shoes

How and Why to Accept Others

Everyone you know and everyone you will ever meet is special and different in some way. The world would be a boring place if people were all the same.

It's our differences that make us all unique and interesting.

When people look or act differently than you, the best thing to do is to try to understand and accept them. In other words, learn more about them, be kind to them, and include them in the things that you and your friends do together.

One great way to try to understand people who seem different from you is to "walk in their shoes."

What does it mean to walk in someone else's shoes?

It means you think about what it would feel like to be them.

- You think about the things that are hard for them and imagine what it would feel like if those things were hard for you, too.

- You think about the things they do and don't enjoy doing and imagine feeling the same way.

- You think about how people talk to them and treat them and imagine how it would feel if people acted in those ways toward you.

After you use your imagination to understand a little more about them and how they feel, you can then treat them how you would want to be treated.

When you take time to understand people and walk in their shoes, you will be showing your kindness, learning about others, and being a good friend!

How are people different from one another?

Here are just a few ways that people can be different from each other:

LOOKS

People look different from each other in all sorts of ways: Some people are tall and others are shorter; some have dark skin and others have light skin; some have long hair and others are bald. You can probably think of many other ways that people look different.

SKILLS

People have different skills and talents—things that they are really good at and that are easy for them to do well. Some people are good at spelling or science. Others might be great singers or good at sports. We all have things that we enjoy doing or that we do really well.

CHALLENGES

People also have different challenges, or things they find hard to do. Some of your classmates may find that learning math takes them longer than it takes their friends. Others might have a hard time riding a bike or playing soccer.

Sometimes these challenges can be small, and people can work hard to improve at the things they find difficult. Other times, these challenges can be bigger and harder to overcome.

FEARS

Everyone feels scared sometimes. Some people don't like the dark and sleep with a nightlight. Others get upset when they see a spider or hear loud noises. The things that scare one person can be different from the things that scare someone else.

PERSONALITY

Some people like to play with their friends all the time. Other people like being alone sometimes, or playing with just a few friends at a time. Some people love to talk and share lots of stories with their friends. Other people might be more shy or quiet.

But even though everyone is different, EVERYONE likes to be included, accepted, and liked!

How are you DIFFERENT?

Here, you get to think about ways that you feel different.

There are many things that I think are fun and that I am really good at doing. One of the things I'm really good at is ....

There are also some things that are hard for me to learn. Some of my friends are good at these things and I wish I were, too. One thing that I think is hard is .... When I can't do that well, I sometimes feel ....

I know that everyone looks different from each other and this is how I think I look different—I am ....

I get scared of some things that might not make other people scared. One thing that sometimes makes me feel scared is ....

I notice that people act differently when they are upset. Some people like to be quiet and alone; others want to be around friends. Some people cry and some people might get mad and yell. When I'm upset, I usually ....

How do YOU like to be treated?

Now, you can think about how you like people to treat you.

When I feel different, I hope that people will: (circle all that apply)

treat me nicely   lend a hand

be my friend   BE PATIENT

NOT LAUGH
AT ME   help me feel
better

You probably circled all of them!

That means that you hope others will take
time to understand you, be kind to you,
and walk in your shoes!

Now it's your turn to learn about people who are
different from you because they have autism. ● ● ● ➤

What Is AUTISM?

Autism is a condition that affects the way some people's brains work.

People with autism are "wired" differently from other people. This means that their brains work differently. As a result, they might not act or behave like everyone else all the time. They are not dumb or wrong, they are just different in some ways—and we've already seen that being different is OK!

Here are some ways that people with autism may act differently:

- People with autism often find it very difficult to communicate. It can be challenging for them to understand what other people are saying. They also find it hard to talk sometimes. Some people with autism may not even be able to talk at all.

- When people with autism have toys, books, or other things around them, they may not seem interested in these things. They also may not use these things in the same ways other people do.

- People with autism often have a hard time making friends or learning how to act around other people.

So you see, some of the things that are easy for you to do—like talking, learning, playing, and making friends—are sometimes very hard for people with autism.

Some people with autism have a problem in
the way their brains deal with the information
that they get from their senses.

People use their senses to experience the world. The five most
well-known senses are seeing, hearing, smelling, tasting, and touching.

All of us feel overwhelmed by our senses sometimes.
Think of yourself and your senses.

- A bright light can hurt your eyes. (Sight)
- A loud noise might surprise you and make you jump. (Sound)
- A really gross smell can make you feel sick. (Smell)
- Very spicy food can make your mouth burn. (Taste)
- When you have a bruise and someone bumps into you, it can really hurt. (Touch)

These things don't bother most people very much.
But some people with autism feel their senses very, very strongly,
so that all the information they are getting from their
senses can become very distracting.

What senses are you most sensitive to?
Answer the questions on the next page to find out.

How do you feel when someone shines a flashlight in your eyes?

....

Can you think of other sights that bother you?

....

....

Can you list three noises that make you want to cover your ears?

1. ....

2. ....

3. ....

What is your least favorite smell?

....

What do you do when you smell it?

....

There are things that you probably find uncomfortable to touch because they feel too hot, cold, sharp, slimy, or rough. What are some things you don't like to touch?

....

....

Is there a certain food that you never, ever want to eat? What is it?

....

....

Everyone has different answers to these questions, because everyone has different things that bother their senses.

Some people with autism have many more things that bother them because they feel their senses much more strongly than you do! Just imagine if there were lots and lots of sights, sounds, smells, tastes, and touches that bothered you and made you feel uncomfortable every day.

Now, I bet you can understand how people with autism might feel overwhelmed a lot of the time.

More About Autism

People with autism need to spend a lot of time and energy working hard to do things that might come easily to you and other people. Many of the things you do every day can be difficult for people with autism.

People with autism usually get help from doctors, therapists, and teachers.

Doctors and researchers are not sure what causes autism or why some people get it. But they do know that it's not contagious—you cannot catch autism like a cold or the flu. So, you don't have to worry about getting autism by spending time with someone who has it.

Many people in the world have autism. Some doctors and researchers think that one out of every 166 people has autism. That's a lot of people.

In this book, we describe autism and some of the common things about people with autism. Remember, no two people in the world are exactly alike, and people with autism are all unique.

▶ Some people with autism have bigger challenges than others and require a lot of help and understanding. These people might have extra help in their classrooms with a personal teacher or assistant. These extra helpers are trained to understand autism. They help to direct, soothe, and teach people with autism in specially designed ways.

▶ Other people with autism may not seem to have as many problems, but they usually still need extra help—especially when it comes to making friends.

▶ Remember, even though people with autism may act differently from you or your other friends, they are special in lots of wonderful ways. And of course, just like you, they have feelings and like having friends.

If you know someone with autism and become their friend, you will both be lucky to have that friendship. You will see that every friendship is different and each one has its own special value!

You and Your Friends with Autism

Understanding what makes them different and
special and how you can be a good friend

You just learned that autism affects how some people's brains work.

When people have autism, it may lead them to act differently than other people.

Now, you will get to learn how and why your friends with autism sometimes act differently.

You can even try to imagine how they feel. Here's your chance to practice taking a walk in someone else's shoes!

Remember, this means you use your imagination to think about how it feels to be them.

Then, you can think about how you can be a good friend to each person you know with autism.

 People with autism may have very good hearing.

Sometimes that may seem good, because then they can hear all sorts of sounds that you don't notice, like faraway cars, birds on the trees outside, or a very soft noise. But sometimes having good hearing means that all of the different noises get really LOUD and distracting to them and it can hurt their ears.

When this happens, they might cover their ears or wear earplugs. They might also say words to themselves so that the other noises they hear don't seem so loud.

Walk in their shoes and see how it feels.

Think about the sound of a fire engine coming down the street and getting louder and louder, and then stopping right in front of you. How would you feel? Noises can be very upsetting, and when they are too loud, you just want them to stop!

Here's another chance to imagine how noises might feel distracting:

Find a place to sit in your school, house, or neighborhood where there are lots of different noises. Write down all the different noises you can hear:

....

....

....

Now, imagine each of these noises getting louder and louder, all at the same time. Can you imagine what it would be like to be very sensitive to all these sounds?

Be a good friend to your friend with autism.

When your friend seems upset about a noise, here are two things you can do: If you are making the loud noise, you can stop making it since you understand that it sounds SO much louder and might be hurting your friend's ears. You can also ask an adult for help if you notice a noise bothering your friend.

 # People with autism may notice many, many details.

Your friends with autism often see a lot of small things that other people don't notice. When they enter a room, they might notice every single color and object in the entire room. They may notice where every picture is hung on the wall, how many desks or people are in the room, and tons and tons of other things.

Since they may see so many things, a situation can sometimes feel overwhelming and cluttered—like a room with a big, huge mess!

So, just like when some people want to clean their messy rooms, your friends with autism may feel more comfortable when everything is put in its usual place.

When something is out of its place, they may become upset. They might cry or do some things that look strange, like flap their hands, twist their bodies, or tap on a desk. They do these things to comfort themselves.

Walk in their shoes and see how it feels.

AlkdjfdlkjfkjfISdlkjfdlkjfdlkdjfkjdITdkjdkjdkjfdkHARDdfkjdkjFOR dkjfdkjfdlkjfdkjfdkjfdkYOUdkjfdkjdkjdkjfTOdfjdlkjfdlkjfREADdlkj dkdkjflkjTHISskjdklkdlPAGE?kdldldDOESkdkdITldldldldlFEELrsr tmsdefjxALL,cvnvwpMESSYdkANDlkdtexjeCLUTTERED?eds hzpdwbgbtetc…Would you like it to be more like a regular page so you do not have to think so hard?

Were you able to read the sentence? Even if you know all the words, they probably became hard to read because they were mixed up with so many other letters. Didn't it feel better at the end, when all that clutter was cleared out so you could just see the words?

Sometimes all the things in a room can make people with autism feel confused and overwhelmed—like you might have felt when looking at this puzzle.

Be a good friend to your friend with autism.

If your friend seems upset because something is out of place, you can ask an adult for help. Sometimes your friend might not be able to use words to describe why he's upset. Maybe he will just point to something and if you think hard and use your memory, maybe you will remember what is out of place.

 People with autism do not like to be surprised—they feel much more comfortable when things are predictable.

Something is predictable when you know it's going to happen because it usually happens in a certain way or at a certain time.

Your friends with autism like to have a schedule or a routine so they know what they are going to be doing every day. They do not like it when things change or surprise them.

If their schedule has to change or if they are surprised by something, they may get nervous, upset, or frustrated. Sometimes they will try to make themselves feel better by doing something over and over again. For example, they might work on a puzzle, clap their hands, or draw a picture. They may not want to stop doing this activity because repeating it makes them feel calmer. They also might go into a corner to be alone and quiet. Sometimes they might talk to themselves or make sounds to help themselves calm down.

Walk in their shoes and see how it feels.

Everyone has routines that they like—things that make them feel safe and comfortable. Maybe you like it when someone in your family says good night to you every night, and you get upset when that doesn't happen. Or, maybe every morning you go to school with the same person and it would be disappointing to you if that changed.

Write down some of the things that you like doing or seeing every day:

....

....

....

Now, think about how you would feel if these parts of your schedule changed.

Be a good friend to your friend with autism.

Since your friend likes to follow routines, you can help her by reminding her about the day's schedule. For example, you might say to her, "In five minutes we'll finish recess and go back inside." That will help her begin to prepare for the change. Or, if something really new happens, like maybe a fire alarm goes off or an unexpected visitor comes to your classroom, you can be patient and understanding. Remember, these new events may be difficult or scary for your friend.

 # People with autism may like to play in different ways than you do.

People with autism often have a difficult time using their imagination. They are much better at thinking about things that are real than things that are pretend.

So when you are playing games where you pretend to be someone else or make believe you are in a different place, people with autism may have a hard time understanding what is going on and joining the game.

Also, they may sometimes forget how to share or take turns.

But just like you, they enjoy playing. Maybe they prefer games with words and numbers, or like playing with puzzles or computers. And like you, they can have fun running around, doing sports, and spending time with friends.

Walk in their shoes and see how it feels.

Can you think of a game or a sport that a friend likes to play but you don't? Can you also think of a game that you find difficult or hard to understand? You might feel left out when your friends are playing games that you don't like or aren't good at.

Now think about how much you appreciate it when other people agree to play games or do things that you enjoy.

Can you remember a time when someone made you happy by playing a game you wanted to play? Write about it here:

Be a good friend to your friend with autism.

If your friend is not playing with anyone, maybe it's because the game doesn't make sense to him. Or if he's playing by himself, maybe it would be nice if you tried his game with him for a while.

If your friend is not doing a good job of sharing with you or letting you have your turn, you should be extra patient, since you know that he is not trying to be mean. It's OK to tell him that you'd like to take a turn.

Sometimes, your friend with autism might sit with you and play, but not talk to you. You should know that even if he doesn't say it, he likes it when you spend time with him.

 People with autism may sometimes have a hard time talking.

People with autism sometimes find it hard to talk or find the right words to say. Some people with autism may not speak at all. They may stay quiet, hum, laugh, or scream. These people might learn how to communicate by using pictures instead of words, or they might use sign language.

Other people with autism do talk, but they may get stuck or confused in a conversation. At times they might repeat certain words over and over.

When your friends can't find words to express themselves, they might get very quiet, walk away from you, or make sounds that aren't real words.

Sometimes if you say something to them, they may just repeat back what you said, instead of answering you.

What time is it?

What time is it?

Walk in their shoes and see how it feels.

Pretend you are in a class and you can't talk. You have to go to the bathroom, but the rule is that you can't go unless you ask the teacher.

How would you ask the teacher without using words?

Would you point down the hall to where the bathroom is? Or draw a picture of a toilet on a piece of paper? Or try to pull the teacher toward the bathroom to show where you want to go?

If the teacher did not understand you or got impatient with you, that would be pretty frustrating, wouldn't it?

Can you imagine how frustrating it would be to know what you want, but not be able to say it?

Be a good friend to your friend with autism.

If your friend doesn't want to talk, don't be hurt, since you know that he might just be frustrated.

You can help your friend when he seems stuck in a conversation by suggesting some words for him to use. If your friend is repeating what you say, remember he is not teasing you or mimicking you—he is just stuck.

Sometimes, just letting your friend know that you want to understand him can be a huge comfort to him. If your friend is struggling to say something and is getting upset, you can tell him that you can see he wants to tell you something and that you will try to figure it out with him.

You can also help him learn words. The easiest way is to show him what you are saying. For example, if you say the word "inside," you can show him what "inside" means by putting a piece of paper inside a box.

 People with autism may
not understand the way
you use certain words.

People with autism think and listen very logically and literally. This means that when they hear statements, they tend to think the words mean exactly the way they sound. But often, other people use expressions that don't mean what they say.

 You probably know that when someone says, "That is so cool," they are not talking about the temperature of something. If someone says, "Can you lend me a hand?" you know they are not actually asking to borrow your hand and take it home.

People with autism may not understand when you use words in a way that is different from their normal or exact meaning. If people around them are using words or expressions they don't understand, they might get frustrated. They might seem confused, upset, or even scared.

Walk in their shoes and see how it feels.

Look at the expressions below. Think about how hard it might be to understand these statements if you always thought that words only had their normal meanings.

Watch out for the ball—duck!   Did you change your mind?

Let's hit the road.   Wow, that's neat.

Can you think of other expressions that use words in this way?

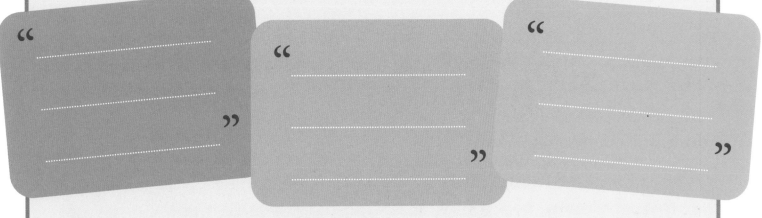

People use these kinds of expressions ALL the time, so just think how often this must frustrate your friends.

Be a good friend to your friend with autism.

When you are talking to your friend with autism, try to avoid using expressions that she might not easily understand. If you say something that seems to confuse her, you can ask if she knows what you mean. If she says, "no," then you can re-word it and try to say it more simply and clearly. When you make the extra effort to choose words with more care, it can make a big difference to your friend with autism.

⭐ People with autism have difficulty understanding nonverbal communication.

Nonverbal communication is the way that people show how they are feeling without using words. Talking is not the only way people communicate with each other.

Sometimes the expressions on people's faces say something about what they are feeling. Smiling, frowning, or shaking your head are all ways you communicate without talking. People also communicate by the way they say things. For example, if people yell it might mean they are angry or frustrated. These things all offer clues to how people feel and they are all parts of nonverbal communication.

It is hard for people with autism to understand these clues. This means that they may not realize how someone around them is feeling or they may not understand some situations.

Since it can be really upsetting to feel confused, people with autism might do some things to comfort themselves. They might clap their hands, rock back and forth, or cover their ears in frustration.

Also, they might not look directly at you when you are talking to them. That's because the expression on your face doesn't help them understand your feelings or what you are saying.

Walk in their shoes and see how it feels.

Look at the pictures below.

You can tell the first boy is happy because you notice that he is smiling. You can also tell that the second boy seems upset because he looks sad. You can guess their feelings by looking at them.

Maybe you will smile at the first boy and comfort the second one.

People with autism, however, might look at these boys and see something that looks more like this:

They won't know HOW to respond because they can not easily figure out what the boys are feeling.

 ## Be a good friend to your friend with autism.

If your friend seems to be ignoring your feelings, don't let this upset you or make you mad. Remember, it may be that he just doesn't understand how you are feeling.

Since your friend may not understand your nonverbal communication, try to use words to explain things.

 People with autism may feel touch in different ways than you do.

Sometimes their skin is very sensitive and even just a light touch may feel like a pinch.

When someone touches them, it may hurt, so they might yell, cry, or sometimes hit back.

Other times, their skin might not have much feeling and they can forget how strong they are. Then, they might be a little too rough when they touch or play with others.

Walk in their shoes and see how it feels.

Think about the last time that someone tickled you. Now, imagine that each of those tickles felt more like a strong pinch.

How does it make you feel when someone pinches you?

What do you do when someone pinches you hard?

 Be a good friend to your friend with autism.

Since your friend may be sensitive to touch, she might not like to be surprised by someone touching her. So, before you touch her, you can ask her if it's OK, or give her some notice so she won't be startled.

If your friend never likes to be touched, don't touch her.

You can still play with her. Just remember that sometimes when you touch her it may hurt and she might get upset.

If your friend is playing too rough, tell her to please not touch you. You can explain to her that she is strong and is hurting you. If she continues to be rough, ask an adult for help.

Friends Value Friends!

Just like with any friend, there are lots of reasons to admire and value your friends with autism. There are many things about them that make them special and good friends.

If you know people with autism, this is your chance to celebrate the great things about them that make them special to you!

What are some things that you admire and value about your friends with autism?

My friend Alice is very special because she works really hard at things. Some things that are easy for other people are a lot harder for her, but she always keeps trying and that is really cool!

My friend knows a lot about trains and I like it when he teaches me about them.

More Questions?

You've just learned a lot about autism and how people with autism might feel in different situations. But you know that everyone is different, so each person with autism may feel and act different ways.

An important part of being a friend is learning all you can about your friends.

Here's your chance to learn even more about your friends with autism.

If you know someone with autism, you may have more questions. Maybe you wonder about how he or she feels about some things or what he or she likes or dislikes. You can write down your questions here:

Here are some other questions that you might want the answers to:

- What games do you like to play?

- What makes you happy?

- What makes you sad?

- What are your favorite subjects in school?

- What can I do to be more helpful?

Now, ask an adult if you should ask these questions directly to your friend or if you should ask a teacher, your friend's parents, or someone else.

You and your friends can **LEARN** more about autism and even do some things together to **HELP** people with autism.

Here are some group activities:

Teach and Learn

If someone in your class or neighborhood has autism (or another special need) you probably want to learn even more about it. You and your friends can go to the library and do research. Then each of you can write a report about the things you learned and present it to your class.

Raise Money for Research

A wonderful way to show that you care about people with autism is to help raise money so that doctors, scientists, and teachers can do more research about autism. You and your friends can make drawings, paintings, and crafts. Then, you can set up a stand to sell the art. Donate the money you collect to a charity for autism.

Communicate Through Pictures

You have learned that some people with autism sometimes have trouble talking. They sometimes might use pictures to express what they want to say.

Here's an exercise where you can practice communicating in a new way.

Each person should find a partner. Sit with your partner and without talking, try to tell your partner what you did last weekend. You can draw pictures—you just can't use any words. Your partner should then tell you what he or she understood from looking at your pictures.

Each person should take a turn drawing to "tell" about their weekend while the other person tries to figure out what their partner is "saying."

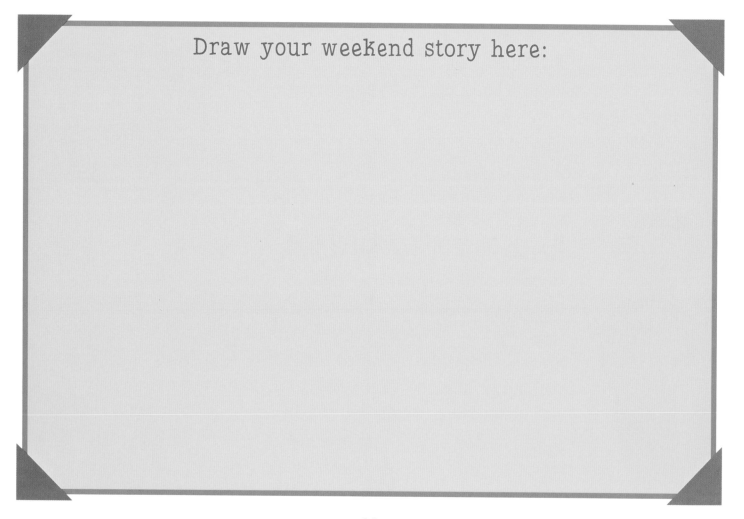

Draw your weekend story here:

Different is Special!

For this activity, everyone should sit in a circle. Each person should take a few minutes to think of something about themselves that is different and special. It can be a hobby, a talent, or anything else about them that is unique. Once everyone has thought of a special thing about themselves, it is time for the group to share their thoughts with each other.

One by one, each person in the group will explain what makes them different or special.

It's nice to see how we are all proud of the things that make us unique!

Compliment Each Other

Now, since everyone likes hearing nice things from others, go around the circle one more time. This time, instead of telling the group something about yourself, give the person next to you a compliment about what makes him or her unique.

The compliment can be something specific such as "I love your red hair," or "You are really good at math." It can also be more general, like "You always treat people nicely."

Doesn't it feel nice to know that the people around you like that you are different?

Here's a Social Story

You've learned that your friends with autism have a hard time dealing with unexpected situations. This can make doing new things seem really scary for them. Can you imagine how it would feel to go to a new school, or go to the zoo or a baseball game for the first time if you were nervous about new things?

One way to make it easier for your friends with autism is to tell them what to expect before they do something new. A "social story" gives them information about what to expect and how to act during a new and unfamiliar situation.

Sometimes social stories are written as lists and other times they use pictures.

Here's an example of a social story for someone who is going on his or her first plane ride. Your friends with autism will read the list to prepare for the new experience.

1. I am going on vacation and I will ride on a plane.
2. I will go to the airport.
3. At the airport it is important to stay with my family.
4. I might have to wait to get on the plane.
5. I will walk through a hallway to get on the plane.
6. I will find my seat and put on my seatbelt.
7. When the plane takes off, it will go fast, get loud, and shake. That's OK.
8. My ears might feel funny. I can ask for gum.
9. In a little while I might get to pick a drink and I might get a snack.
10. When the plane starts to land my ears might feel funny again.
11. The plane will get loud and might be bumpy.
12. I will keep my seatbelt on and my hands down until the plane stops.
13. I might have to wait and then I will get off the plane.

Now it's your turn. On the next page, you and your friends can write a social story!

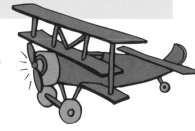

Create a Social Story

Write a social story for your friend who is going to the movies for the very first time. Remember that he is very sensitive to many things, so the more details you give, the better. It will also help if you explain to him how he should act.

1.
2.
3.
4.
5.
6.
7.
8.
9.
10.

EXPRESS Yourself

Your AUTISM ACCEPTANCE JOURNAL and SCRAPBOOK

We're leaving the next couple of pages blank for you.

Here's why: We know we didn't think of everything. You probably have other ideas about how to use these pages!

You can:

Write a story about a time when a friend of yours included you when you felt left out or different.

Make a list of cool ideas and projects that you can do with your friends to raise money to donate to autism research.

Describe how it feels to be around one of your friends with autism. Write about the ways your friend makes you happy or the special things about this friendship.

Write a letter to the president or your senator that asks him or her to support giving money for autism research.

OTHER STUFF

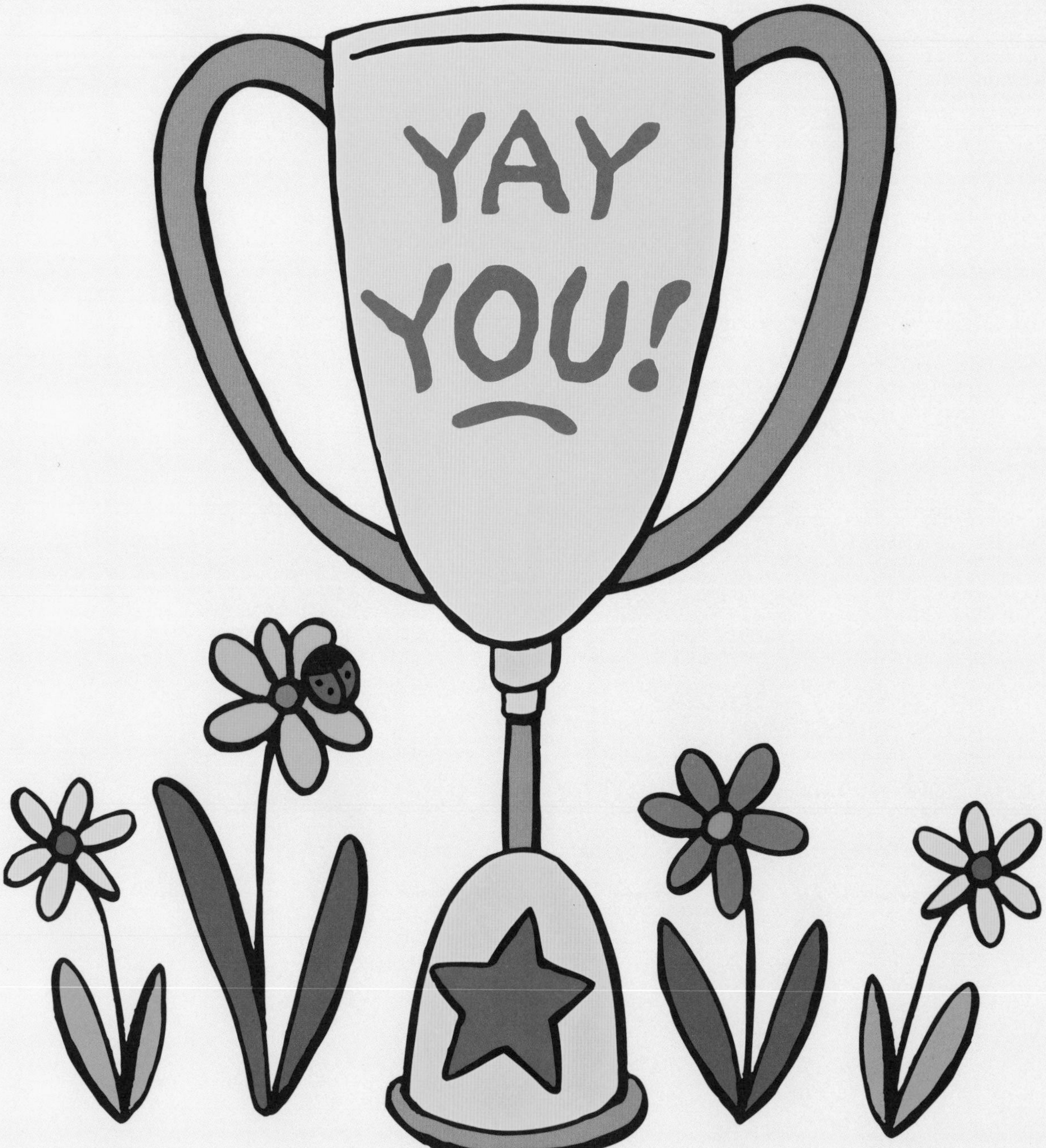

Congratulations!

You've learned a lot about autism. This AUTISM ACCEPTANCE BOOK certificate shows that you take time to understand people and learn how they are different and special. That makes you special, too!

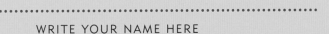

THE AUTISM ACCEPTANCE BOOK

This certificate is awarded to

....

WRITE YOUR NAME HERE

for learning to walk in other people's shoes so you can understand them and be a good friend.

....

DATE

Now it's your job to spread the word!
Tell your friends and family how important it is to try to understand, accept, and include everyone.

Reference Ideas for Adults

There are many good sources of information for adults who are teaching children with autism, for parents of children with autism, and for adults seeking to teach children how to be tolerant and accepting of others.

Some organizations that focus on autism:

Autism Speaks: www.autismspeaks.org

Autism Society of America: www.autism-society.org

Cure Autism Now: www.cureautismnow.org

National Alliance for Autism Research: www.naar.org

Each of these organizations offers additional resources such as books, websites, support groups, and experts.

Other Resources:

The local PTA might have a special committee (called a SEPTA, or Special Education PTA) that has information for parents of children with special needs, including listings of specific resources in your area.

Parent Training and Information Centers and Community Parent Resource Centers in each state provide training and information to parents of children and youth with disabilities and to professionals who work with children. This assistance helps parents to participate more effectively with professionals in meeting the educational needs of children with disabilities.

The Technical Assistance Alliance supports these programs and offers many useful links and resources: www.taalliance.org/centers/

Teach Others to Accept People with Autism!

We'd love you to tell others about The AUTISM ACCEPTANCE BOOK.

Go to www.wateringcanpress.com to:

● Order additional books for children you know or to donate to an organization of your choice,

● Learn about bulk purchases for schools, youth groups, stores, or organizations,

● View the free AUTISM ACCEPTANCE BOOK Teacher's Guide, and

● See other Watering Can® series books.

Have fun and do great things
with **THE GIVING BOOK**!

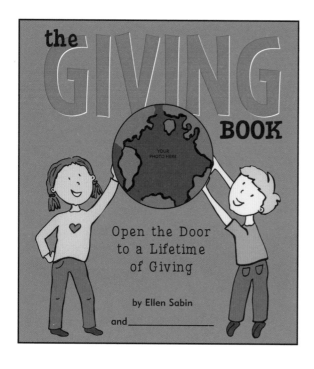

The GIVING BOOK is a really fun way to…

- Think about your wishes and dreams for making the world a better place!

- Appreciate how you feel when people are kind and giving to you.

- List all the different things you have to share with other people, like your talents, your time, and the things you have.

- Do fun activities with your family or friends to help other people. You can even do things to help animals or the planet.

- Learn ways to save money to give to your favorite charities or organizations.

- Realize how powerful your actions can be and how much of a difference you can make in the world!

The **GIVING BOOK** grows kids with character.

It is an activity book, a journal, and a scrapbook that inspires and records a child's journey into a lifelong tradition of giving and charity.

Be a hero and enjoy
THE HERO BOOK.

The HERO BOOK lets you think about the people you admire and the things that make you a hero, too!

The HERO BOOK lets you:

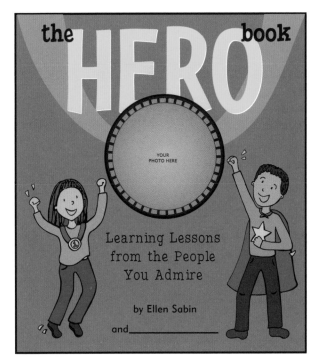

- Consider the qualities you admire in others.

- Write stories about people who show courage, fairness, acts of kindness, or who possess other admirable traits.

- Think about well-known heroes from history or everyday heroes from your own life.

- Write about what you learn from your role models.

- Think about the things that make you a hero to others!

The HERO BOOK grows kids with character.

It is an activity book, a journal, and a conversation-starter that spark and records a child's journey into finding role models who will inspire them to be their best.

The Giving Book and **The Hero Book** are offered with free teacher's guides for use in classrooms. Free guides are also available for parents, youth groups, or others to use with the books in social settings. Find these free resources at www.wateringcanpress.com.

We hope that you have
learned a lot about autism
and understanding people who
are different than you.